HARDPRESS.NET
HOME OF HARD-TO-FIND BOOKS

Semiramis, a Tragedy
by George Edward Ayscough

Address:
HardPress
8345 NW 66TH ST #2561
MIAMI FL 33166-2626
USA
Email: info@hardpress.net

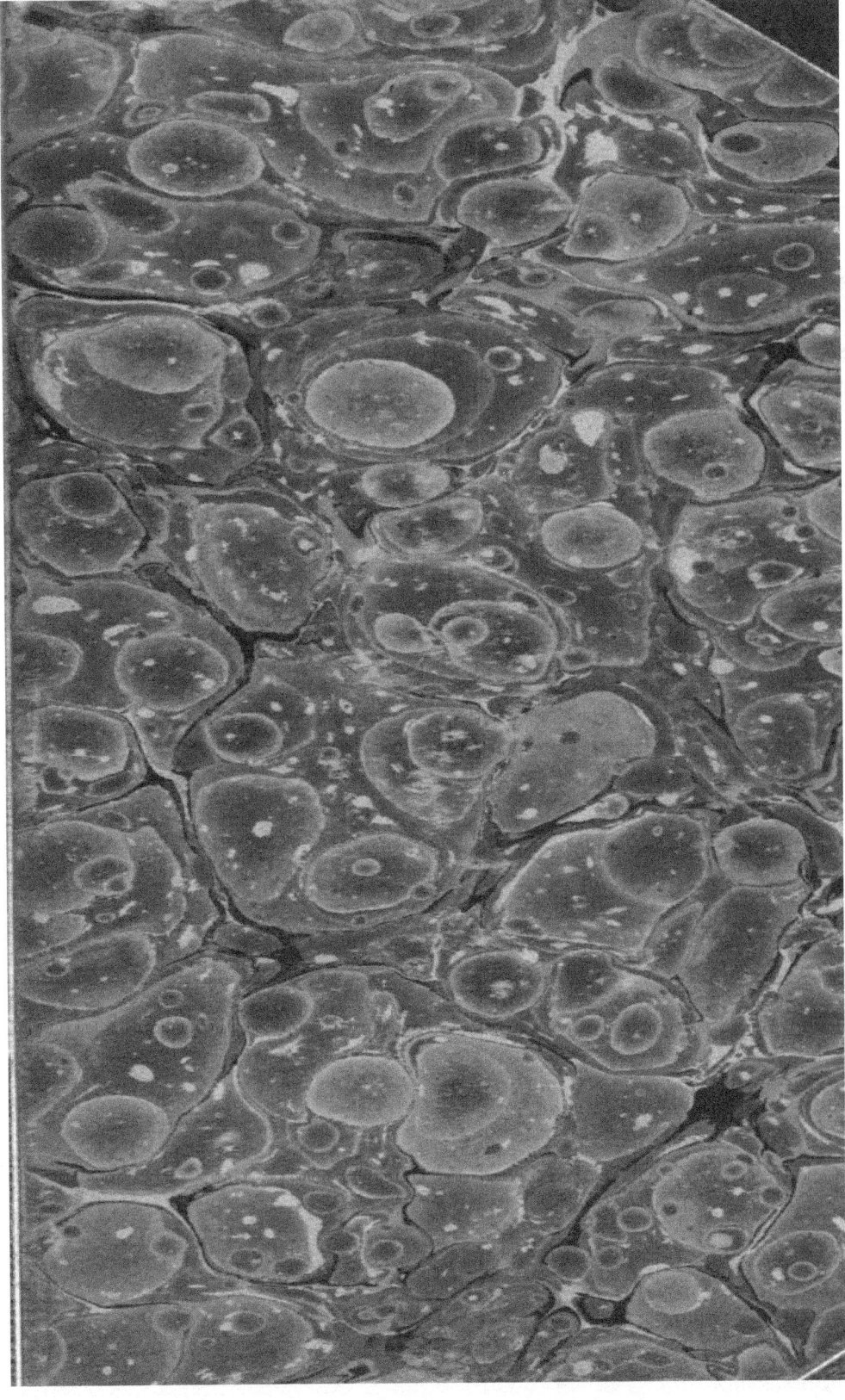

FORTI NIHIL DIFFICILE

Coningsby Disraeli. D.L.
Hughenden Manor House.

Shuttleworth 276.

from the Author

SEMIRAMIS,

A

TRAGEDY:

AS IT IS ACTED

AT THE

THEATRE ROYAL

IN

DRURY-LANE.

By GEORGE EDWARD AYSCOUGH, Efq.

LONDON:

PRINTED FOR J. DODSLEY, IN PALL-MALL.

M.DCC.LXXVI.

T O

Sir *James Cockburn*, Baronet,

AS A LITTLE TRIBUTE

OF FRIENDSHIP AND GRATITUDE,

THIS TRAGEDY

IS INSCRIBED,

BY HIS MUCH OBLIGED,

AND MOST AFFECTIONATE

BROTHER-IN-LAW,

AND VERY HUMBLE SERVANT,

George Edward Ayscough.

PROLOGUE.

Written by G. E. AYSCOUGH, Esq.

Spoken by Mr. REDDISH.

CRITICS! *I come your favour to implore*
For one, who never quak'd so much before!
He, for a while, has left the gay parade,
Has doff'd the gorget!—and the smart cockade!
Each instrument of war has thrown aside,
To fret! and strut it here—in tragic pride!
From foreign shores are rich materials brought,
Which to your English *mode our Bard has wrought.*
Phœbus forefend—lest he new dangers run,
And rise, like Icarus, *too near the sun ;*
On waxen pinions just about to sink,
On his own rashness then too late he'll think,
And drown in a black *sea of———critic's ink !* }

Ye gentle, feeling, female hearts be kind !
A soldier sues !—his brows with laurels bind !
In this—your empire, your protection yield !
At life's expence—he'll pay you in the field *!*
Nor fighting battles, nor besieging towns,
He dreads !—and only trembles at your frowns !

But hold !—our Author bad me say one word
To all his honour'd brothers of the sword !
He begs by them this night to be befriended ;
And bids me promise, (this great bus'ness ended)
He'll gladly re-assume the Sash *once more,*
If they his pristine rank will then restore, }
Nor deem him a deserter *from the* CORPS !

DRAMATIS

DRAMATIS PERSONÆ.

ARZACES,
OR
NINIAS,   } by Mr. SMITH.

ASSURES,   Mr. BENSLEY.

OROES,   Mr. REDDISH.

MITHRANES,   Mr. GRIST.

OTANES,   Mr. FARREN.

CEDARUS,   Mr. CHAPLIN.

SEMIRAMIS,   Mrs. YATES.

AZEMA,   Miss HOPKINS.

SEMIRAMIS.

ACT THE FIRST.

SCENE THE FIRST.

In Front the Palace of Semiramis *appears, with the Gardens raised above it on lofty Terraces; on the Right Hand is seen the Temple of the Magi, and on the Left a vast Mausoleum adorned with Obelisks.*

Enter ARZACES *and* MITHRANES.

ARZACES.

YES, my Mithranes, by expreſs command,
 In ſecret iſſued from the throne itſelf,
Behold your friend in Babylon's proud walls!
—— Ye powers, how all theſe wonders that ſur-
   round us
Strike my aſtoniſh'd ſenſes, and imprint

B

A faint

A faint idea of her noble foul
Who plann'd thefe brilliant fcenes, thefe maffy
     tow'rs !
See where yon temple rears its facred head !
See yon fair gardens in the air fufpended !
View next, with reverence, this monftrous pile
By fond affection rear'd to her lov'd lord,
This dark abode of Ninus !——O Mithranes !
Thefe are immortal works, inferior only
To her who rais'd them ! divine Semiramis !

          M I T H R A N E S.

Raife not thus high your hopes, warlike Arzaces,
Leaft when you view this phœnix of her fex,
Grief fhould ufurp the place of promis'd joy.

        A R Z A C E S.

How's this ?

        M I T H R A N E S.

     The Queen, alas ! a prey to forrow,
Here vents thofe griefs that rend her tortur'd
     breaft ;
One while fhe fills the air with direful fhrieks,
One while fhe mufing, fad, and filent, fits,
And looks like her whofe fenfes are o'erthrown
By moping melancholy ;——then again
She ftarts ! and bends her fteps towards thefe fhades,
Sacred to night, to filence, and to death,
And kneeling near the afhes of her lord,
She beats her breaft, tears her difhevel'd hair,
And calls on Ninus, and her long-loft fon.

         A R Z A C E S.

ARZACES.

Since when has angry Heaven thus o'erwhelm'd
    her?

MITHRANES.

Alas 'twas then, even in that hour of joy,
When Babylon with grateful shouts proclaim'd
Your high deserts,
When they enraptured gazed on fair Azema,
Her whom your valour had but newly freed
From Scythian ravishers, and barb'rous bonds;
Then, when within this ancient city's walls
No sounds were heard but those of varied mirth,
Of revelry and joy—then did the Queen,
Like some fair flower, wither in her prime,
And droop without one chilling, wintry blast.

ARZACES.

Thou mov'st my wonder—but perchance Azema
Shall work a cure; one pray'r of her's to Heaven,
Shall calm the rage of the offended gods.
Yet say, my friend, is the Queen ever thus?

MITHRANES.

Not always; for oft-times her tow'ring spirit
Breaks from the galling shackles of affliction;
But when again she sinks beneath the load
Of these oppressive ills—her royal hands
Let loose the reins of empire;—and Assures,
That haughty prince, that shame of Belus' race,
Wielding the scepter of the woe-worn Queen,
Makes ev'n the nobles groan beneath his yoke,

While

While all the empire feels his iron rule.

ARZACES.

By various dangers fee me now environ'd !
The traps, the wiles, the poifon'd fnares of courts,
And who fhall now direct my erring fteps ?
Who wifely curb or check th' impetuous rage
Of youthful paffion ?——Once I had a guide,
A friend, a counfellor, a tender parent,
But oh they're loft for ever ; ravifh'd from me,
And now lie buried in thy tomb, Phradates.

MITHRANES.

I cannot blame thy grief —— you're caufe to
     mourn
The pious fage Phradates, —— Ninus lov'd him,
Alas my royal fovereign dearly lov'd him,
And to his care and breeding did intruft
His and this kingdom's hope —— the youthful
     prince.
Thou know'ft it was thy fire's unhappy lot
To have furviv'd them both, from which fad hour
He bad farewell to courts, and freely fought
An honourable exile——Thou alone
Of all mankind, didft reap a bleffing from it;
For thou didft catch inftruction from his lips ;
He taught thee how to tread the paths of virtue,
The way to greatnefs, and the road to heaven.

ARZACES.

I read not yet my fate within thefe walls :
'Tis true my fword has triumph'd in the war,

And

And when Semiramis impos'd her laws
O'er conquer'd nations, on the Oxine shores,
From her victorious car a look she cast,
A look of favour on my growing fame.
But 'tis not so in courts ; transplanted there
The soldier languishes, is there thrown by,
While slaves and silken cowards rule above him.
All this my dying sire has oft declared,
And has moreo'er in mystic language told me
My fate depended on the common cause.
That charge he then deliver'd to my care,

[*Pointing to a casket.*

Which long he kept conceal'd from eyes pro-
     fane,
He bad me trust it to the hallow'd hands
Of Oroes the pontiff, who alone
Its value knew, and could unfold its worth.

MITHRANES.

Deep is the holy science of this priest,
By him the mysteries of Fate and Nature
Are fathom'd and explored ;————but in his func-
     tion,
As in his holy vestments, he's involved ;
Free from ambition, and from worldly views :
He places not his mitre next the crown,
You view him near the altar, not the throne.
Yet will I penetrate yon sacred fane,
And call him for a while from holy cares,

               That

That thou may'ft execute thy pious truft,
And do the will of thy dead fire before him.

                                      [Exit.

SCENE THE SECOND.

A R Z A C E S *folus.*

And yet methinks 'tis ftrange, that I, a foldier,
Bred up in camps, and train'd to deeds of blood,
Should by my dying father be call'd forth
As one moft fit for this myfterious work !
Now too, when love warming my youthful heart
Stamps me his vot'ry, now do I deferve
To be the bearer of thefe holy off'rings,
To altars, priefts, or our Affyrian gods ?

SCENE THE THIRD.

To him enter the High Prieft OROES, *attended by other Priefts, and* MITHRANES,

M I T H R A N E S.

Behold, my lord, this noble youth's arrived,
And brings thofe relics which you feem to await !

A R Z A C E S.

Moft holy prieft of thefe Caldean fhrines,
O do not deem their fanctity profaned
By a rough foldier's prefence, hither borne
To obey the mandate of his dying fire,

                                     And

And lay this sacred casket at your feet.
——————You loved my father.

OROES.

Brave and warlike youth,
I loved the many virtues of Phradates;
But 'tis the gods', and not thy father's will,
Have sent thee here. Say, where's thy sacred
trust?

ARZACES.

——Behold it here.——
[*Two slaves deliver the casket to the Priest.*

OROES.

Is it then ye I touch,
Ye ever dear remains? do I once more
Bedew you with my tears? Thanks to the gods!
——Retire, my friends, and leave us here alone,
I have a sacred mystery to unfold.
[*Exeunt Priests.*
Behold the seal,
The seal of empire, which proclaim'd the laws!
And this sad scroll, traced by his dying hands!
This diadem, which crown'd his royal brows!
Lo here the sword, which overthrew the Mede,
And bent the Persian to the Assyrian yoke!
But all proved useless to its mighty lord,
'Gainst perfidy, 'gainst death, in lurking poi-
son.——

ARZACES.

Oh all ye powers!——Poison!

6   OROES.

OROES.

Yes, Arzaces!
Long has this dreadful fecret been enwrapt
In tenfold night, fafe kept within my breaft;
But now the manes of a murder'd king
Refume new life——Th' offended gods themfelves
Now cry for vengeance, and their voice is heard
Loud iffuing thro' the marble jaws of death.

ARZACES.

Thy words are full of horror, as of truth.
Laft night as wand'ring near this facred fpot,
Too fure I heard fhrieks and heart-rending
     groans,
As 'twere within that tomb——

OROES.

           The groans of Ninus——
Thy flaughter'd fovereign groans for juft revenge.

ARZACES.

Yet, Pontiff, fay, from whom does he expect it?
Or who fhall execute his great commands?

OROES.

The traitors who cut off this beft of kings,
Have kept conceal'd all traces of their plot,
Their guilt lies buried here within the tomb:
Men's wifdom is o'er-reach'd, their eyes deceiv'd,
But who fhall blind th' all-piercing eye of
     Heaven?

ARZACES.

ARZACES.

I would this hand were doomed the inftrument
To punifh thefe fell crimes. When I beheld
That fatal tomb, and heard thofe awful founds,
My fpirit was difturbed——Is it not lawful
To enter here?

OROES.

Stri&ly the gods forbid it,
The oracle has otherwife decreed;
But wait with patience for the hour of juftice,
That hour fhall come, and the high hefts of
   Heaven
Shall be perform'd——The Fates now clofe my lips,
They will unfeal them at the appointed time,
Then more may be divulged——Perchance, O youth,
It may concern thee nearly——but be watchful
Leaft any a&ion, word, or look of thine,
Betray this dreadful fecret of the tomb.
——Behold the palace opens——proud Affures,
Attended by a train of courtly flaves,
Enters the royal dome——prepares t'infe&
With baneful flattery our mifled Queen.
O thou fell monfter!——haughty, fubtle villain!

ARZACES.

What fays my lord?

OROES.

No more——Farewell!——
Bear hence thofe facred relics; and when night
O'erfhades thefe guilty walls, again we'll meet,

C   Again

Again hold converſe in the awful preſence
Of liſt'ning gods ;——learn to revere them, youth,
For ſtrictly do they watch thee.

                         [*Exit* Oroes.

SCENE THE FOURTH.

ARZACES *ſolus*.

                   Wherefore me ?
Curſt be this ſpot where mighty Ninus fell !
Curſt be the hand which mix'd the deadly
     draught !
——Yet why conceal this wretch ?——Methought the
     prieſt
Levelled a foul ſuſpicion at Aſſures.
——How now, my friend ?

SCENE THE FIFTH.

To him enter MITHRANES.

MITHRANES.

              Retire, moſt noble youth ;
Aſſures, ſprang from Babylonian kings,
The haughty fav'rite of our ſovereign, comes :
All here reſpect and dread him — you yourſelf,
Ev'n without diminution of your glory,
May pay that deference which his ſtate demands.

                       ARZACES.

ARZACES.

Thou counselleſt ill, I will not ſtoop to him;
Nor ſhall my crouching aggrandiſe his pride.

SCENE THE SIXTH.

Enter ASSURES, *followed by* CEDARUS *and*
Nobles.

ASSURES.

How's this——Arzaces here ! at Babylon
Without our leave obtain'd ?——Say, daring youth,
Whence ſprings this boldneſs ? wherefore have
      you left
Your camps and ſtandards on the Oxine ſhores ?
And what wild motive brings you to the court ?

ARZACES.

My ſervices have borne me here, nay more,
The Queen's high mandate. ——

ASSURES.

            How ? the Queen require !——
—— Well, be it ſo —— but know from me alone
Thou can'ſt obtain admiſſion to the Queen.
What wouldſt thou with Semiramis ? ——

ARZACES.

                              I dare
To aſk the bright reward of all my toils,
And humbly ſue to ſerve her. ——

ASSURES.

Thou dareft more,
Thou doft conceal thy moft prefumptuous love,
Thy paffion for Azema. ——

ARZACES.

Yes, I own
It is prefumption to adore that maid,
For I efteem her heart, at which I aim,
Beyond the worth or price of empire.

ASSURES.

Hold.
I hope thou know'ft not whom thou dar'ft infult,
Or could'ft thou hope to mingle thy vile race
With demi-gods o' th' Tigris and Euphrates.
—— Yet I will deign thro' pity to advife thee.
When thou behold'ft the Queen, I charge thee, youth,
Drop not one hint of this thy offenfive love,
Not on thy life——Thou'ft heard, and now obey.

ARZACES.

Now reft affured, proud lord, I'll urge my fuit
With double vigour —— I defpife your threats,
For menaces ftill ftrengthen my refolves.
Behold in me one who has ferv'd the ftate,
Whofe arms may have oft protected you, proud lord,
And all the filken train within the palace.
You deem me rafh, perchance, this fire offends,
But it fhall ne'er be ftifled——nor fhall you

E'er

E'er teach my neck t'endure a flaviſh yoke.

ASSURES.

I will chaſtiſe this inſolence—and thou
Shalt learn the duty of a ſubject.——

[*Exeunt* Aſſures, &c.

ARZACES.

Well,

We both may learn it; I henceforward
May learn more prudence, nor again be laviſh
Of theſe wild tranſports of my headſtrong ardor;
While you may one day prove how great the peril
Even for proud ſtateſmen to inſult the man
Whoſe arms have triumph'd in his country's
cauſe.

[*Exit* Arzaces.

END OF THE FIRST ACT.

ACT

ACT THE SECOND.

SCENE THE FIRST, *continues.*

*Semiramis appears leaning on her Woman, as in the
deepeſt Affliction:—at length ſhe comes forward,
followed by Otanes.*

SEMIRAMIS.

OH that the friendly hand of death would
     caſt
His darkſome veil o'er theſe unhappy eyes,
Grown dim with tears, and weary of the ſun!
—Is not Arzaces yet arrived ?

OTANES.

                    He is ;
This day, O Queen, he enter'd theſe proud walls.

SEMIRAMIS.

'Tis well—for know, Otanes, this dread voice
Piercing the ear of night, has warned thy Queen,
That when Arzaces ſhould arrive, her woes
Should meet a reſpite, and her torments ceaſe.

OTANES.

Shall not theſe tidings then diſpel this gloom,
And ſtop the current of theſe endleſs tears ?

SEMIRAMIS.

They form a ray of hope, my ſoul methinks
Will loſe its terrors in Arzaces' preſence.

                         OTANES.

OTANES.

Banish all recollection of that deed,
Which freed you from the fatal marriage yoke;
The act was almost justice, for the King
Had basely driv'n you from his bed and throne;
And sure the various blessings you've diffused,
Join'd to the grateful prayers of many nations,
Shall plead so strongly at Heav'n's high tribunal,
That were the gods incensed at Ninus' death,
They'd blunt the sword of vengeance. —— See
     Assures,
His crime surpasses yours, he mix'd the draught;
Yet prosp'rous still, rejoices in his greatness,
Nor dreads, nor feels the anger of the gods.

SEMIRAMIS.

Alas! my guilt was greater, as my ties
Were far more sacred, for I was the wife
Of murder'd Ninus, and my fix'd despair
Accuses me to all the pow'rs of vengeance.
I once had hopes, that when my darling son
By untimely death was torn from my fond arms,
Vengeance divine had ceas'd; but since this phan-
     tom,
This dreadful vision, has disturb'd my peace,
I often seek that tomb, revere from far
The ashes of my lord, invoke his shade,
Then shrieks, long and loud groans answering
     my vows,
Seem to foretell some dire event.—Perchance
                 The

The hour's now come to expiate my crime.

OTANES.

Might not your sorrow conjure up this spirit?
Perchance the offspring of your troubled mind?

SEMIRAMIS.

Too sure thefe eyes beheld it—'twas no child
Of fancy or of sleep, for sleep has long
Fled from thefe eyelids—Wakeful on my bed,
Pondering on my fad lot, I heard a voice
Exclaim " Arzaces !" at which name did joy
Dawn on my heart, that heart which curft Affures
Has pierc'd with horror; for I hop'd Arzaces
Might dare t'oppofe him, and his pow'r reftrain,
Who, as the foul accomplice of my crime,
Afpires to fhare my fcepter;—for an inftant
My forrows coas'd, when lo in Ninus' form
Sudden the minifter of death appear'd,
His threat'ning fword befmear'd with clotted
        blood.
Methinks ev'n now I view the injur'd fhade,
Methinks I hear him groan !

OTANES.

            Say, mighty Emprefs,
What did the fhade reveal ?

SEMIRAMIS.

            He would not fpeak
His direful purpofe; therefore I remain'd
In dark fufpence, dreading uncertain ill,
A ftate fo curft—the heavy load of life

9   Grew

Grew irksome ;—thirsting then to know my fate,
And dreading to consult the sainted pontiff
Whom Babylon reveres,
Proudly disdaining that a priest should view
His monarch trembling in a mortal's presence,
I sent to Memphis to consult great Jove,
With gifts and incense, tho' too well convinc'd,
That neither gifts nor incense can atone
For crimes so great as mine.

OTANES.

Oft do these oracles direct the steps
Of erring mortals.——

Enter MESSENGER.

MESSENGER.

Great Queen, the Egyptian pontiff is arriv'd.——

[*Exit* Messenger.

SEMIRAMIS.

I go to meet him.——May the gods remove
The veil 'twixt me and fate, and may I read
My destiny to come ! whether I'm doom'd
To sink beneath my suff'rings, or find
A period to my sorrows in Arzaces.

[*Exeunt.*

D

SCENE

SCENE THE SECOND.

ARZACES and AZEMA.

AZEMA.

To you, Arzaces, this unconquer'd empire
Its present splendour owes, and I my freedom;
For when the vanquish'd Scythians, to repair
Their late defeats, sprang with their treacherous
    bands
Forth from their gloomy caves and dark retreats,
With rage redoubled rushing on our troops;
Then when my warlike father fell, and left
In hopeless slavery the lost Azema,
You sent the furious thunder of the war
Beyond their desart's bound'ries, and your hands
Unloos'd her chains, and satisfied her vengeance,
Vast is the debt I owe you, and this heart's
Your poor reward.

ARZACES,
    Must I not claim this hand?

AZEMA.

It ne'er shall be another's;—but take heed
Least this our mutual passion prove our ruin.
O let me warn you, that this martial pride,
Joined to the lover's softness, may destroy us,
They both alike incense a dangerous rival,
Too great t' oppose or cope with—vile Assures.

ARZACES.

ARZACES.

Is then that infolent, ambitious man
My rival as my foe?

AZEMA.

'Tis true, ambition lords it o'er his mind,
He pants for royal power, and feeks my hand
Fafter to grafp the fcepter in his own.
But truft me, my Arzaces, if the prince,
He whom great Ninus deftin'd from his birth,
Would wed Azema; if this empire's heir
Were yet alive, and in his mother's court,
If with his diadem his heart he proffer'd;
I call the confcious powers of love to witnefs,
I would difdain them both, and would prefer
Exile with thee, before a throne with him.

ARZACES.

Benignant gods! 'tis now that I am bleft:
While thus I triumph in Azema's heart,
How much I foar above th' ambitious hopes
Of fell Affures!——

AZEMA.

　　　　Yet let me conjure you
To dread his vengeance, which will know no
　　bounds
Towards his love's rival——whom, from other mo-
　　tives,
Ev'n now he hates, and labours to deftroy.

ARZACES.

I hate him more, but ne'er can learn to fear him.

The

The Queen between us, with moſt even hand,
Doth poize the balance of her royal favour.
Soon as I proſtrate fell before her throne,
With her own hand ſhe rais'd me from the earth,
And oft ſhe call'd me her victorious ſoldier,
Her kingdom's beſt ſupport.   Yes, my Azema,
I heard my praiſes iſſue from thoſe lips,
Which mightieſt ſovereigns glory to obey.

AZEMA.

Theſe tidings cheer my heart; for if the Queen
Deigns to protect, in vain Aſſures threatens.

ARZACES.

Embolden'd by her goodneſs, at her feet
I meant t' implore her to complete our union.
But ere I ſpoke, behold a prieſt approach'd,
Bearing great Ammon's oracle.   The Queen
With trembling hands unſeal'd the ſcroll, let
    fall
Some precious tears, and fix'd her watry eyes
Long time on me, with marvellous attention,
Then ſigh'd, and fled my ſight.   What this
    ſhould mean
I know not; yet I deeply mourn her fate.

AZEMA.

Leave her not to Aſſures, and his counſels;
He may prevent her good intents.
My pray'rs ſhall aid my wiſhes and my hopes;
I feel in loving you I pleaſe the gods.
Now let the vanquiſh'd Eaſt fall down and worſhip
                    Divine

Divine Semiramis——I am more great;
The world is at her feet, but you at mine.

ARZACES.

Behold the traitor comes !——at his appearance
My foul is feized with an unwonted horror.

SCENE THE SECOND.

Enter ASSURES.

ASSURES.

It feems on thee high honours have been lavifh'd,
For which ev'n kings themfelves have figh'd in
      vain.
Nay, thou haft dar'd prefumptuoufly to rival
High-born Affures in Azema's love.

ARZACES.

I've learnt, it's true, to honour and revere
That race from which you fprang, your rank and
      blood ;
But in defpite of all thefe rights you boaft,
I dare put in my claim, I love the maid ;
And I could add, if like a peaceful courtier
I chofe to vaunt before her, I upheld
That throne which you, Affures, hope t' afcend.
And now I hafte t' obey Azema's orders.
By her and by Semiramis alone
I am commanded. You perchance hereafter
May wield the fcepter, but ne'er hope to rank
Arzaces in the number of your fubjects.
              Thou

Thou may'ft be king——for oft the gods in wrath
Do monarchs give as fcourges to mankind.

[*Exit.*

SCENE THE THIRD.

AZEMA *and* ASSURES.

ASSURES.

His infolence too long has been endured.
But may I now hold converfe with Azema,
On fubjects far more worthy her attention ?

AZEMA.

Can there be theme more glorious ? Speak, my
    lord,
I am all attention.

ASSURES.

O let no trifling cares ufurp your thoughts,
The world's great guidance, univerfal fway
Shall foon call on us, and fhall occupy
Each vaft idea.——Lo ! Semiramis
Is but the fhadow of herfelf, high Heaven
Seems to debafe her greatnefs, and that ftar
Which long has fhone with undiminifh'd blaze
The glory of our hemifphere, has loft
Its wonted luftre, and now hafting on
Towards its decline, fhall fet in endlefs night.

AZEMA.

My lord, I am not fkill'd in ftate intrigues,
But know not why you deem yourfelf impower'd
To tax my fighs, or read my virgin thoughts.

5   ASSURES.

ASSURES.

Cherifh afpiring thoughts, thoughts worthy
    kings.
The fate of empire hangs upon our union:
For now I fpeak to mighty kings and heroes,
And all the demi-gods from whom you fprang.
Too long a woman trampling on their afhes,
Ufurping pow'r to which we fhould lay claim,
Has held enthrall'd the nations of the earth.
Complete the work then of her falling greatnefs.
Time was, fhe had your charms ; affume her
    courage.
Love fhould not dare prefent himfelf before you
In aught but in a monarch's form. That crown
I tender, and I truft you'll not prefer
A rude barbarian ?

AZEMA.

Peace, peace, Affures.
Shall I contemn the glory, and difgrace
The names recorded by eternal fame
Of my great anceftors ? Though I deny
That in the blazon of that glorious ftrain
One could be found of more exalted foul,
Than him you dare mifcall a rude barbarian.
For me, when Fate decrees that I muft wed,
'Tis for Semiramis to guide my choice.
You fay the gods are all incenfed againft her.
I know not for what crime ; but this I know,
That thou wilt never be the chofen man,

                Th

The holy feer commiffion'd by the Fates
To point the thunder of avenging Jove.   [*Exit.*

SCENE THE FOURTH.

Manet ASSURES.   *To him enter* CEDARUS.

ASSURES.

Well, faithful Cedarus, fay, what fuccefs?
Say, will the feeds of hatred and rebellion
Which we have fown in men's diftemper'd bofoms,
Will they fpring up, will they ere long bring forth
The fruits of difcord and inteftine war?

CEDARUS.

I dare hope much, my lord——at length the people
Break their long filence, and, imprefs'd no more
By that dread awe in which the vaunted name
Of great Semiramis had bound their fenfes,
They now demand to know this empire's heir;
Say they muft have a king to hold their fcepter,
And that Semiramis muft name Affures.

ASSURES.

O fource of endlefs fhame!——muft then my glory,
My rank, my very fate, depend on her?
Was it for this, ye powers, I murder'd Ninus,
And, wading deeper thro' the fea of blood,
Cut off his infant fon, and fo removed
My only barrier to th' Imperial throne?
Have I done this to crawl in Babylon,
To be a fubject?

CEDARUS.

CEDARUS.

Check th' ignoble thought.

ASSURES.

Spite of myfelf I am compell'd to praife her;
For, Cedarus, I've feen this godlike woman,
When the vaft empire like a drunkard reel'd,
And as a coward fhook with rude commotion,
Into her hands take the disjointed rule,
With the fharp fword of juftice mow oppreffion,
Stop all the various fources of corruption,
Silence the murmurers, ftifle the tumults,
And with fuch art and wifdom mould the ftate,
That peace and order have embrac'd each other.

CEDARUS.

But now her genius grovels in the duft.

ASSURES.

Behold in me a mighty minifter,
But robb'd of power ; a prince but without
        fubjects ;
Encircled with high honours, yet dependant.
But woe befall her, if th' ungrateful woman
Drives to extremes her defperate confederate.

SCENE THE FIFTH.

To them enter OTANES.

OTANES.

My lord, the Queen requires your private ear.

E   ASSURES.

ASSURES.

Lo! she appears! Retire good Cedarus.

[*Exit* Cedarus.

SCENE THE SIXTH.

To him enter SEMIRAMIS.

SEMIRAMIS.

My lord, at length I must unfold that heart
Which in your presence has absorb'd its grief.
I've govern'd Asia, and perhaps with glory;
You too have borne the weight of this vast em-
    pire.
Long have I liv'd so blest, that I forgot
The dreadful step which rais'd me to this height.
I was unmindful that the gods were just.
But now Heaven speaks, I yield, and this great
    kingdom
Will soon be strengthen'd, even from its foun-
    dation.

ASSURES.

It is a part that's worthy of my Queen
To finish this her glorious work——but say,
What power is able to obscure that glory?
The earth obeys you, what d'ye fear from
    Heaven?

SEMIRAMIS.

Can you ask this, while you behold yon tomb?

ASSURES.

ASSURES.

I muſt confeſs I cannot bear with patience
To be reminded that once Ninus reign'd.
For fifteen years that king has ſlept in peace,
And do we fear his ſhade ſhould burſt the tomb,
And come thus late to cry to man for vengeance?
No fears like theſe ſhould ſhake your daring ſoul;
But if 'tis now intent on nobler plans,
If you'd perpetuate the blood of Belus,
If fair Azema's claim to this high rank——

SEMIRAMIS.

Aye, that's my theme——Great Jove, and Babylon,
Demand without delay the ſcepter's heir,
And I muſt chuſe a partner of my throne.
You know my pride, and my unconquer'd
        ſpirit,
Have made it long their law to reign alone;
But now Heaven's voice aſſiſts my people's
        prayers,
I muſt divide my power——'Tis you, my lord,
Who beſt may claim the title of a king;
You're next in power on earth, but not my equal.
It is enough, and I've the pride to think
That rank may ſatisfy your vaſt ambition.

ASSURES.

Great are your favours, Queen, great my deſerts;
For you I've dy'd my hands with royal blood,
And ſhall I not receive the bright reward
Of this bold deed?

SEMIRAMIS.

Hear
Great Ammon's oracle, and know my will.

[*Reads.*]
" All Babylon fhall wear a face of joy,
" When the fad mother, and more cruel wife,
" Shall light once more the Hymeneal torch.
" Then fhall fhe calm the reftlefs fhade of
" Ninus."

Such are the eternal orders of the gods.
This day, I mean to give the world a lord;
My choice may fall on you, or on another,
In all things I'll affert my fovereign power,
But chiefly in this act.—Do you give orders
The princes and the magi ftrait affemble.
This day the offended gods fhall be appeas'd,
But 'tis repentance only can difarm them;
And truft me, that remorfe which you defpife
Is the laft virtue which the guilty boaft.
You deem me weak and timid, but alas
Fear ever dwells with crimes. This very fear
Adds luftre to my crown — and 'twould become
    thee,
Humbling thyfelf, to deprecate Heaven's ven-
    geance.   [*Exit.*

SCENE

SCENE THE SEVENTH.

Manet ASSURES.

I muft not wed Azema — for the Queen
Fixes on me to fhare her bed and throne.
What all my pains, join'd to our mutual crimes,
Could ne'er effect, behold an idle dream,
And an Egyptian oracle, bring forth !——
What power unknown directs the deeds of mor-
    tals !
What feeble fprings act on our great defigns !
Still muft I doubt. —— Once more I'll fee the
    Queen,
Strive craftily to read her dark intents,
Watch all the fecret workings of her foul,
And from her great refolves arrange my own.
                      [*Exit.*

END OF THE SECOND ACT.

ACT

ACT THE THIRD.

SCENE THE FIRST.

A Royal Gallery in the Palace.

Enter SEMIRAMIS *and* OTANES.

SEMIRAMIS.

WHO would believe, Otanes, that the gods,
    Offended as they are at my tranfgreffions,
Would deign to fhed a ray of comfort round me,
And cheer with hope my dark, defpairing foul?
The hand of Heaven has led Arzaces hither;
Doubtlefs 'tis they difpofe of human hearts;
And mine exults t' obey their facred laws.
My fate is fix'd, I yield, and I behold
Mine and the world's great mafter in Arzaces.

OTANES.

In him! in young Arzaces?

SEMIRAMIS.

                Yes, Otanes.
When Perfia was reveng'd, and Afia conquer'd,
This hero fought on the rude plains of Scythia;
Surrounded as he was by death and carnage,
And crown'd with laurels, yet his youthful front
Was crimfon'd with the blufh of modefty.
At the firft glance of this young hero's charms,
Wonder and joy feized on my aftonifhed fenfes;

                                        All

All other men were objects of my scorn,
While something seem'd to whisper to my soul,
To favour and protect him from this instant.
This did not 'scape the cunning of Assures,
He hates the noble youth—whose glorious image
Was 'graven on my heart, long ere I knew
That Heaven had doom'd him to partake my
   throne.

OTANES.

Is it decreed then that your daring spirit,
Your proud unconquer'd heart, at last should
  yield ?

SEMIRAMIS.

No—'tis not love inclines me toward Arzaces;
I pay to beauty the reward of valour.
Is't for a wretch like me, to yield to love ?
To own its fatal laws, and court its bonds ?
Hast thou forgot, that I was once a mother ?
Hast thou forgot, that scarce these wretched
   arms
Embrac'd the fruit of my unhappy union,
When Heav'n in anger tore him from my bosom ?

OTANES.

The world has long bewail'd the prince's loss.

SEMIRAMIS.

Mankind had cause to mourn—what then had I ?
I fled my court, I wish'd to fly myself;
I sought repose amidst these sacred tombs,
But rest fled from me—now with joy and wonder
         I see

I fee foft Peace return to cheer my foul;
The gentle goddefs comes, and with her brings
Divine Arzaces, to difpel my forrows.

OTANES.

This deed of thine, O Queen, will caufe the heart
Of proud Affures to o'erflow with rage.
The people's voice, joined to his own ambition,
Have taught him long to cherifh the fond hope
That he fhould prove your choice.

SEMIRAMIS.

                        I've not deceiv'd him,
And know, Otanes, I difdain to fear him.
I am no ftranger to his tow'ring views,
But ftill I've fet due bounds to his ambition.
What fhall I dread then?——fhall he dare t' oppofe
Semiramis, united with Arzaces?
'Twould prove an infult to the facred fhade
Of my dead lord, to wed with his affaffin.
The oracles of Jove approve Arzaces,
And Ninus quits the bofom of the tomb,
To urge this union.——Now no more I'm aw'd
By the fuperior virtue of the pontiff;
I bad him ftrait attend to know my will.

OTANES.

The holy prieft approaches——he'll declare
If this your choice be pleafing to the gods.

                        [Exit Otanes.

                        SCENE

SCENE THE SECOND.

Enter OROES *to* SEMIRAMIS.

SEMIRAMIS.

August fucceffor of great Zoroafter,
This day I mean to name the Affyrian king;
'Tis yours to place the diadem on his brows.
Is all prepar'd for this folemnity?

OROES.

The magi and the nobles are affembled;
Your will is done, and there my duty ends.
I'm bound to obey, but not to judge our mo-
　　narchs;
That tafk is fitting only for the gods.

SEMIRAMIS.

Thefe obfcure phrafes, this myfterious language,
Shew that in fecret you condemn my choice.

OROES.

I know it not—O may it prove a blefs'd one!

SEMIRAMIS.

The oracle demands a facrifice.

OROES.

True, mighty Queen; Ammon fhall be obey'd.

SEMIRAMIS.

Say, venerable pontiff—have the facred altars
This morn receiv'd the off'rings of Arzaces?

F　　　　　　　　　OROES.

OROES.

They have, O Queen,—and Heaven doth hold
    them precious ;
He and his gifts are pleasing to the gods.

SEMIRAMIS.

I do believe thee—and thy sayings, priest,
Do cheer my soul.—May I not trust Arzaces?

OROES.

He is the firmest pillar of the state;
The gods have led him hither, and his glory
Is their own work.

SEMIRAMIS.

            With joy, with heart-felt transport
My ears imbibe these tidings—Hope and peace
Shall calm ere long the tempest in my soul.
Haste, and let all your altars smoke with incense,
Your holy roofs resound with notes of praise.
And strait do thou and all the magi join
In supplications to the gentle gods
To shed their choicest blessings on these nuptials.
                              [Exit Oroes.

SCENE THE THIRD.

Manet SEMIRAMIS.

SEMIRAMIS.

The gods smile on me while I chuse Arzaces.
Thus I become the minister of Heaven.
How will this sudden, this unhop'd-for greatness,
                              Fill

Fill his aftonifh'd foul with joy and wonder !
How will Affures and his minions droop,
When ev'n the man whom moft they hate fhall
    rule them !

SCENE THE FOURTH.

Enter O T A N E S.

O T A N E S.

Arzaces waits your will.

S E M I R A M I S.

           Bid him approach.
Ye gods, defenders of the Affyrian throne !
Who now infpire me, and direct my deeds :
Thou reftlefs fpirit of the murder'd Ninus,
And thou, O bleffed fhade of my dead fon,
Unite your powers, and favour my Arzaces.

SCENE THE FIFTH.

Enter A R Z A C E S. *Kneels before her.*

A R Z A C E S.

O Queen, my life's devoted to your fervice,
I owe you all my blood.   When I've beheld
Its purple drops gufh forth, I've been o'erpaid,
Since 'twas for you it flow'd.——My warlike father,
Leading your troops to conqueft, fell in battle.
But wherefore dare I to remind my fovereign

                F 2   Of

Of my dead father's merits ?——Will she therefore
Deign to forgive the rashness of his son,
Who even now thus prostrate at her feet,
Dreads to offend her, and to urge his suit ?——

SEMIRAMIS.

Rise, Arzaces !
Thou surely ne'er wast born to give offence.
Dismiss thy fear, and boldly name thy suit.

ARZACES.

This day, O Queen, you give your hand and em-
        pire ;
The proud Assures now prepares to triumph ;
Hither ev'n now he bends his haughty steps,
As 'twere to claim the conquest.   The whole
        realm
Have fix'd on him, as sprang from your high
        blood,
To share your throne ; —— may he prove worthy
        of it !
But O, I feel my mind is too exalted
Here to adore the man whose power I've braved.
Suffer me then to fly his hated presence,
And seek that land where late I fought your
        battles.
Tho' I might well defy his tyranny,
If you, O Queen, would crown my aspiring
        wishes
And grant me————

                                SEMIRAMIS.

A TRAGEDY. 37

SEMIRAMIS.

Gracious powers! what do I hear!
Would'ft thou then fly my court? Say, would'ft
    thou leave me?
And can'ft thou dread Affures?

ARZACES.

          No—I'm doomed
To fear nought elfe on earth, except your anger.
But now perchance my vain defires are known,
Your indignation may deftroy my hopes,
I tremble——

SEMIRAMIS.

    Thou haft no caufe—ere long you'll find
Affures is not deftined for thy fov'reign.

ARZACES.

'Tis well—for I muft own, with ten-fold horror
I fhould have feen him fill the throne of Ninus.
But fince 'tis now forbad him to afpire
To thefe auguft efpoufals, is't decreed
That he muft therefore wed the fair Azema?
Pardon, O Queen, th' excefs of my prefumption.
Tho' but a fubject—yet 'gainft him I durft——

SEMIRAMIS.

Subjects like you, are pillars to my throne.
My eyes are now enlighten'd, and I view
What tends to the true interefts of the ftate.
I name you arbiter; you fhall fupport them.
My word fhall break the concord 'twixt the
    princefs

                   And

And proud Affures——Truft me, I've forefeen
And will prevent the dangers of this union.

ARZACES.

And fhall this curft alliance then be broken?
Now I perceive thy penetrating wifdom
Reads my defires, and dives into my foul.

SEMIRAMIS.

Here break we off——ere now the hall of audi-
ence
Is fill'd with nobles, and Affyrian princes,
Follow, Arzaces : let us hafte to join them,
And witnefs with them my auguft decifion.

[*Exeunt.*

SCENE THE SIXTH.

*The Scene draws and difcovers a large magnificent Sa-
loon. Many of the great Officers of State enter in
Proceffion, bearing the Marks and Enfigns of their
Dignity——then enter Oroes, with the other Priefts
——A Throne is raifed in the Midft of the Salloon, on
which the Queen having feated herfelf, is furrounded
by Azema and her Women. The Satraps are placed
next the Throne, with Affures and Arzaces,
Guards and Attendants.*

OROES.

Princes ! priefts ! warriors ! Babylon's fupport !
Here by the Queen's command this hour affembled,

To

To you great Jove's decree shall be reveal'd.
The gods themselves watch o'er this mighty em-
    pire;
And now the great, the important day's arriv'd,
Which they have destin'd shall new mould the
    state.
He whom the Queen shall deem most fit to
    rule,
He whom she chuse to share her bed and throne,
Our part is to obey.——Lo, in the name
Of all the magi do I bring that homage
Due to our monarch——prayers, and pious vows,
For her own safety, and this kingdom's welfare.

A Z E M A.

Ev'n now, my Lords, the Queen shall name your
    sovereign.
Th' imperial choice can injure only me ;
But I was born her subject, and remain so.

A S S U R E S.

Whate'er may be the mystic will of Heaven,
Who this auspicious day directs our monarch;
We're bound t'obey——Swear we then by this
    throne,
And by the name of great Semiramis;
Humbly to yield to her sublime commands,
To own 'tis justice, to submit in silence.

A R Z A C E S.

I swear——and this my arm, and my good sword,
With every drop of blood within these veins,

                I de-

I dedicate henceforth to my new King,
With that same duty, and that heart-felt zeal,
With which they long have strove to serve my
    Queen.

O R O E S.

We wait the will of Heaven, and our Sov'reign.

S E M I R A M Í S.

Princes, and ye most holy priests, attend.
If now for more than fifteen years the world,
Fill'd with my glories and my great exploits,
Has seen, and has rever'd, the sword and scepter
Placed in a woman's hand, ev'n in that hand
Which tyrant custom, and the laws of Ninus,
Had destin'd to the distaff;—if alone
(Surpassing ev'n my subjects' fondest hopes)
I have sustain'd the weight of this vast empire,
Throughout the world victorious and adored,
I've scorn'd t' accept a partner in my greatness;
Yet now this empire shall acquire new force,
Since, in obedience to great Jove's decree,
I deign to give my hand, and share my power.
I might have chosen a husband from the kings
Whose states surround the borders of my realms,
But they're my tributaries, or my foes.
My scepter is not made for foreign hands;
My subjects are far greater in my eyes
Than all these petty kings, which their brave arms
Can conquer and enslave;—therefore this hour
My diadem shall bind a subject's brows.

    3

Say,

Say, is there one amongst you who presumes,
Ev'n though in secret, to condemn my purpose?

ASSURES.

No, mighty Queen, all must applaud the deed,
And own the wisdom of their monarch's choice.

SEMIRAMIS.

Belus was born a subject, and his crown
He ow'd to his own merits, and his people:
'Tis by those very rights that now I reign,
And sway a mightier scepter.—I have taught
Full twenty eastern Kings to own your laws,
Nations far distant, and unknown to Belus;
It was for me to finish his great works.
And now, my people, you demand the hero,
Worthy to rule this wide-extended empire,
Worthy his subjects, and the hand that crowns
      him.

ARZACES.

With deference we wait your great commands.

SEMIRAMIS.

Sages, and legislators of the land!
The oracle of thunder-bearing Jove,
The welfare of this state, the world's great in-
      terest,
All these have I consulted; they decree
This union shall effect a general good,
And shed unnumber'd blessings on mankind.
Haste and adore this hero who shall rule ye;
In him the princes of my race revive:

G   My

My hufband, and this monarch is——Arzaces.
    [*She defcends from the throne, and they all rife.*

AZEMA.

O perfidy! Arzaces!

ASSURES.

        O for vengeance!

ARZACES *to* AZEMA.

Truft me, my love, my faith's inviolate.

OROES.

        Juft Heaven, difpel thefe horrors!

SEMIRAMIS *to the Priefts.*

O ye, who fanctify the pureft vows,
Now plight our faiths, and join our willing
    hands.   [*It thunders.*

OROES.

Break off thefe rites, for Heaven itfelf frowns on
    them.
Depart we, mighty Emprefs; on this inftant
Seek we great Ninus' tomb, and to his fhade,
Strait offer pious prayers, with vows and in-
    cenfe.   [*Exeunt the* Queen *and* Arzaces,
                         followed by Oroes.

The Scene fhuts.——*Manent* ASSURES *and* AZEMA, *&c.*

AZEMA.

Gods, is it poffible! is this the prince
So warlike, fo renown'd? is he confederate
With a deceitful Queen and crafty Prieft?
And will they dare ufurp the name of Heav'n
To give fome colour to their dark proceedings?

6   ASSURES.

ASSURES.

Such is their plan; and reft affured, fage prin-
    cefs;
'Tis meet we fhould compofe our amorous broils,
And re-unite thefe hands, which this rough fol-
    dier
Has, by his prefence, rudely torn afunder.

AZEMA.

Say I fhould yield, what good fhall thence accrue
To poor Azema?

ASSURES.

Afk you this, bright maid?
Our mutual ftrength and pow'r will prove too
    ftrong
For this bold youth to oppofe——and fhou'd the
    Queen
Vainly prefume to uphold her daring ruffian,
She then will feel what 'tis to infult Affures.
But can Azema lofe her fex's pride?
Can fhe forget her youth, her charms difgrac'd?
Say will not this infpire a cold contempt,
And teach her heart to feel its mighty wrongs?

AZEMA.

Alas! the traitor takes my lover's part,
And fain wou'd cherifh the falfe hopes he gave
    me.

ASSURES.

Away with love, when love repays it not;
'Tis the mind's ficknefs, worthy vulgar fouls.

Azema,

Azema, fprung from heroes and from kings,
Shou'd foar above her fex's common views.
Her every wifh fhould comprehend a world;
Empire and univerfal fway her object?
Such do I bring, fuch offer to her beauty;
Nay more, the godlike joy of juft revenge!

AZEMA.

Revenge! ye pow'rs, on whom? on my Arzaces!
Alas, my perjur'd love! ambition may
Cancel thy vows, tho' regifter'd in Heaven;
Unfhaken ftill, mine fhall defy its power.
Be falfe and fafe, 'tis man's prerogative;
But let Azema prove her fex's virtue,
And faith, tho' injur'd, triumph over falfehood.

[*Exit.*

ASSURES.

Curfe on the wayward fex, fhe loves him ftill,
Nor can my arts fubvert her girlifh paffion.
Then be it fo; fure means fhall be employ'd.
True politicians firft effay to gain
Their fav'rite points by ftratagem and cun-
　　ning;
Yet difappointed, never quit their aim,
But boldly re-affume the road of pow'r.
Come then Revenge! Ambition fire my foul!
At once be all its feelings gratified.
The ftripling who has dar'd to brave my ven-
　　geance,
This hour fhall feel it; and with heart-felt tranfport
　　　　　　　　　　　　　　　　　　　　I'll

I'll give him death, and mount the throne of
    Ninus.   [*Exit.*

Scene opens, and discovers the Tomb, at which are
   SEMIRAMIS, ARZACES, *and* OROES.

SEMIRAMIS.

Yet, Oroes, hold; for wherefore shou'd we pause
To know Jove's will, for what his oracle
So late declar'd.   This hand is thine, Arzaces.
And now I charge thee by thy function, Pontiff—
    [*It thunders, and the shade of* Ninus *appears.*
It is the voice of Jove; he speaks in thunder.
See, the tomb opens, and the hallow'd shade
Of my dead lord bursts forth !—I faint—I die.

ARZACES.

Lo where I stand !—look down, O sacred phantom,
Speak, and reveal thy terrible commands.

SEMIRAMIS.

O speak thy dreadful errand. Art thou come
To pardon or destroy ?—
Judge if this hero well deserves thy crown.
Pronounce, I am bound t' obey—

SHADE *to* ARZACES.

                  It is decreed
That thou shalt reign, Arzaces; but thou'rt
    doom'd
To expiate first fell crimes and blackest treasons.
There is a sacrifice thou must perform
Here in my tomb, and to my sacred ashes,
                      And

And ſerve thereby me and my ſon——be mindful
Of thy dead King, and liſten to the Pontiff.

ARZACES.

Bleſt Shade, whom I revere, whoſe matchleſs
    ſpirit
Inhabits yet, and animates theſe climes,
This thy ſtrange viſitation doth not ſhake
My ſoul with fear, but fills it with new ſtrength.
And here I ſwear to do thy ſacred will,
Tho' peril, or the death, await the act.
Speak hero, demi-god——O name the taſk
To which this arm is deſtin'd.——

SEMIRAMIS [*kneels.*]
                 Mighty Ninus,
Suffer thy wife thus proſtrate on the earth,
If deep contrition, and if heart-felt ſorrow,
If I've not ſinn'd beyond all hopes——

SHADE.
                   Forbear;
But reſt aſſur'd the hour now haſtens on
When 'twill be lawful for thee to deſcend
Into this houſe of death.

    [*He re-enters, and the Mauſoleum cloſes.*

SEMIRAMIS.
              Haſte, Pontiff, haſte !
Bid all the magi follow to the temple ;
Speak comfort to my people, calm their fears !
My huſband's manes yet may be appeas'd,

                         They

They favour me since they protect Arzaces.
The gods inspire me, Ammon names your King.
Do present sacrifice, let victims bleed!
And with fit orisons implore great Jove
To bless that monarch he himself hath chosen.

[*Exit.*

END OF THE THIRD ACT.

ACT

A C T T H E F O U R T H.

S C E N E T H E F I R S T.

Enter A R Z A C E S *and* A Z E M A.

A R Z A C E S.

O Add not to the burthen of my woes
By thy severe reproaches and complaints.
This oracle is more replete with horror
Than thou conceiv'st.——Astonish'd nature groans
With endless prodigies——While my own grief
Lays heavy on my soul, the cruel gods,
Have ravish'd from me all my fondest wishes;
I have lost Azema——

A Z E M A.

Cease, thou perjur'd man,
Cease to increase the horrors of this day,
By bringing thy false love to my remembrance.
I do not mean to oppose the hand that crowns thee,
Much less to thwart the sacred will of Ninus.
Of all the prodigies I've this day seen,
That which most tends to freeze my soul with
horror
Is thy inconstancy, thy barbarous falshood.
Complete thy work, say Ninus bids thee strike.
Begin by me thy horrid sacrifice;
Strike, thou base ingrate.

A R Z A C E S.

ARZACES.
          Gods, it is too much.
'Gainft the fharp arrows of all other woes,
Methinks my fad defpairing breaft was arm'd,
But O, what fhield fhall blunt the poifon'd fhafts
Levell'd againft me by Azema's rage?
Judge of my grief at the Queen's fatal choice,
Judge of the precipice to which it drives me.
Now hear what Heaven decrees.

AZEMA.
          I've heard already.

ARZACES.
This empire is not deftin'd to my rule,
Nor fhalt thou fway its fcepter——for the fon
Of royal Ninus, whom I've fworn to ferve,
He who was born my rival and my mafter,
Yet lives.

AZEMA.
     Ye mighty gods! does the prince live?

ARZACES.
He breathes, he lives——ere long he fhall appear
Within thefe walls.

AZEMA.
          And fad Semiramis?

ARZACES.
Thus long deceiv'd has mourn'd for her loft fon.
As yet he knows not this important fecret,
Which has lain buried in the pontiff's breaft.

H   AZEMA.

AZEMA.

Alas, thefe myfteries perplex my foul,
For the Queen weds thee, and the fhade of Ninus
Foretold that thou fhould'ft reign ————

ARZACES.

But Ninus' fon
Is deftin'd for thy hufband.——Who can unfold
Thefe dreadful prophecies, and dark predictions?

AZEMA.

Yet fpeak, declare——why comes he not this in-
ftant?
What fecret myftery conceals the monarch?
Not he himfelf, nor great Semiramis,
Should tempt me to forget my vows to thee,
And by black perjury defile my foul.
And now, Arzaces, deeply probe thy heart,
There read, if thy fond paffion equals mine.
And now farewell——go and receive the fentence
Which angry Ninus threatens to pronounce.
Thy lot depends on Heaven, my fate on thee.

[Exit AZEMA.

ARZACES.

Arzaces is thy own.——Stay, cruel maid————
Methinks my foul's bewilder'd, and I'm loft
In this ftrange mixture of delights and horrors!
But fee where Oroes comes to clear my doubts,
And calm my reftlefs mind!————

SCENE

SCENE THE SECOND.

Enter OROES, *bearing the Offerings of* ARZACES.

ARZACES.

O holy father,
Remove this dreadful darkness from my eyes,
And snatch me from the abyss in which I'm
plung'd.

OROES.

The hour now comes, my son, when that dark veil
Which thus obscures thy sight, shall be remov'd.
Now in his dismal, his profound abode,
Ninus expects thee, from thy hand awaits
The offering, and the destined sacrifice
Reserv'd by fate to appease his injur'd manes.

ARZACES.

O name this offering which his shade demands.
But sure it ill becomes me to revenge
The wrongs of Ninus, while his son survives.

OROES.

'Tis his sire
Who now by me issues his dread commands.
Thy part is to obey. Some half hour hence
Be found near Ninus' tomb, armed with this
sword,
This sacred steel, which well becomes thy hand;
Thy warlike front, bound with this diadem,

H 2 Which

Which heretofore the brows of Ninus graced,
Which thou brought'st hither.

A R Z A C E S,

                But fay, wherefore thus ?
Why with the crown of Ninus deck my tem-
     ples ?

O R O E S.

'Tis fo decreed———.
Within that tomb the victim will be found,
Whofe blood thou haft fwore to fhed——fear not,
     but ftrike,
Great Ninus' manes fhall direct the blow.

A R Z A C E S.

Should he demand my blood I will obey him.
But yet thou fpeak'ft not to me of the young
     prince,
Nor haft thou yet reveal'd from what ftrange
     caufe
Ninus approves that I fhould wed the Queen,
Or how by fuch efpoufals I fhall reign ?

O R O E S.

Thou wed Semiramis !——at thought of this
The infernal powers themfelves turn pale with
     horror.
Now read thy fate, Arzaces.
Know too, that this vile woman———

A R Z A C E S.

             Who, the Queen ?

O R O E S,

OROES.

Cut fhort the thread of her dear hufband's life,
And robb'd the world of Ninus—bafe Affures
Mixt the curft draught, and minifter'd the poi-
fon.

ARZACES, *after a fhort Paufe.*

This crimes fuits the fell nature of Affures.
But can I think this Queen, this wife of Ninus,
So lov'd of nations, fo rever'd by monarchs,
Would e'en attempt a deed more black than
    hell,
And dye her guilty hands in her King's blood?

OROES.

This doubt, O youth, proclaims thy noble foul,
But now 'twould ill become me to diffemble:
Ceafe then to wonder if offended Ninus
Rifes from death, and once again revifits
Thefe guilty walls—he rifes to forbid
This monftrous union—comes to rend afunder
Thefe chains of wedlock by the Furies forg'd:
He comes to fave his fon from horrid inceft.
Hark! now he fpeaks! he warns thee! he's thy
    father—
Thou art thyfelf the prince—the Queen's thy
    mother.

NINIAS.

Thou haft fpoke poniards, prieft!—Wounded at
    once
With all thefe mortal ftrokes—I ftand envelop'd
                                        By

By thefe dark fhades of death, and tenfold hor-
    ror !

Can it be poffible that I am the fon

Of murder'd Ninus ?

O R O E S.

               Thou'rt his royal offspring :

And know, O prince, that when thy godlike
    fire

Perceiv'd the effect of the too fubtle poifon,

And with accumulated grief beheld

That a like baneful and deftructive draught

Attacked the fources of thy infant life,

He fnatched thee dying from this impious
    court.

But while all Babylon deplor'd thy lofs,

Thou waft committed to the pious care

Of good Phradates——who with healing juices

Of plants and herbs known to the Perfian fages,

Expell'd the deadly venom from thy veins,

And having loft his only fon in battle,

He adopted thee, and call'd thee his Arzaces.

N I N I A S.

O loyal act !——he was indeed my father.

What if Affures prove the only traitor,

If he alone were guilty ?

                 [Oroes *giving him a Scroll.*

                   View this fcroll,

Behold thefe facred characters, Arzaces ;

Can'ft thou ftill doubt ?

N I N I A S.

NINIAS.

Give me the writing, and thereby root out
The laft remains of hopes, and flatt'ring doubts.

- [*Reads.*]

" Expiring Ninus to the true Phradates.
" I die by poifon——O preferve my fon,
" Hafte to fnatch Ninias from his murderers.
" My guilty wife————"

OROES.

Doft thou lack further proof?
Thou know'ft 'twas from thy hand that I re-
        ceiv'd
This dreadful teftimony——which the monarch
Had furely finifh'd——but that death approach'd
And froze his feeble hand.——Fear nought but
        guilt.
Go on, brave prince, while thro' this night of
        horrors
The great gods
Themfelves fhall guide thee——Mark'd with Hea-
        ven's feal,
To thee th' immutable decrees of fate
Are now intrufted——yet thou art but mortal,
Ordain'd the feeble inftrument of vengeance ;
'Tis not for thee to interrogate great Jove.
Remember, prince, thou haft been fav'd from
        death ;
Therefore exalt thy voice in grateful praife ;
                              Think

Think what thou ow'ft to Heaven, nor dare to
    murmur.   [*Exit* Oroes.

SCENE THE THIRD.

N I N I A S.

No——nought fhall e'er reftore my priftine peace.
O dreadful thought! Semiramis my mother!

SCENE THE FOURTH.

To him enter Semiramis.

S E M I R A M I S.

The Hymenal rites now wait thy prefence,
Great monarch of the earth —— hafte to the altar,
Thy fate and mine, join'd to the kingdom's
    welfare,
Depend on this our union——Lo, with tranfport
I fee the pontiff's hallow'd hands have placed
That facred diadem on thy brow——fure proof
That Heaven approves, and doth confirm my
    choice.
Even the daring party of Affures,
Struck with religious awe, falls down and trem-
    bles.
The people's hands, their very hearts are ours;
You reign fecurely, and your Queen adores
    thee;
In vain Affures rages.——
        10   N I N I A S.

NINIAS.

Curſt Aſſures,
Why do I thus delay to ſeek the monſter?
Now ſhall he make atonement, and waſh out
The filthy ſtains of parricide and treaſon
In his perfidious blood;——the ſhade of Ninus
Shall be appeas'd.

SEMIRAMIS.

How's this?——the ſhade of Ninus!
Juſt Heaven! I named not Ninus——'twas Aſſures.
Why are thoſe eyes fix'd as in anger on me?
Is this the tender, the ſubmiſſive heart,
Which I ſo fondly hoped thou would'ſt have
     offer'd,
And which from thee had proved a grateful tribute
To her who gave thee empire?
Diſmiſs thy fears of Ninus, and his anger,
And let me find new comfort in thy arms,
My woe's laſt refuge!——my belov'd Arzaces;
My kingdom's beſt ſupport; my lord, my huſ-
     band!

NINIAS. [*turning from her.*]

It is too much; forbear, I charge thee.

SEMIRAMIS.

Why is my lord abandon'd thus to ſorrow?

NINIAS.

Hear me, Semiramis!

SEMIRAMIS.

I'm all attention.

I

NINIAS.

Alas! I've not the power to speak my purpose;
Doom me to death, or fly my sight for ever.

SEMIRAMIS.

For pity's sake, my lord, reveal the cause
Of this disorder in your troubled senses:
The traces of despair are in your visage,
Those fatal glances freeze my soul with horror.
Some unknown power, with force invincible,
Drags me towards you, and at the same instant
Tears me from your embrace, seeming to join
The deadliest terror to the purest love.

NINIAS.

Leave and abhor me.

SEMIRAMIS.

　　　　　Ha! what that writing, that
On which so oft you cast your angry eyes,
And moisten with your tears? Does it contain
The cause of all your woe?

NINIAS.

　　　　　Too sure it does.
Dar'st thou peruse it?

SEMIRAMIS.

　　　　　Wherefore should I fear?
Whence hadst thou it?

NINIAS.

　　　　　It was the gift of Heaven.

SEMIRAMIS.

Whose characters are these?

NINIAS.

NINIAS.
They are—my father's.

SEMIRAMIS.
What fay'ft thou ?

NINIAS.
Tremble !

SEMIRAMIS.
Let me read my fate.

NINIAS.
Forbear—each word's a poniard to thy foul.

SEMIRAMIS.
I care not—thou fhalt folve my dreadful doubts.
If ftill thou doft refift—I deem thee guilty.

NINIAS.
Great gods, who guide my deeds, 'tis ye who
force me !
Take it—and may the pangs which it fhall
caufe,
Prove the fole punifhment which heavenly juftice
Referves for thy high crimes.

SEMIRAMIS.
What do I fee !
Support me.

NINIAS.
'Tis reveal'd.

SEMIRAMIS. [*after a long filence, recovering.*]
It is my fon !—Delay not—but fulfil
Thy deftiny. Now do the work of Fate,
Punifh this guilty, this accurfed wretch,

I 2

Revenge

Revenge thy father's moſt unnatural murder ;
Prove thou art his ſon, and pierce thy mother's
  breaſt.

N I N I A S.

O ſooner ſhall my ſword drain the laſt drop
Of that unhappy blood which flow'd from thine ;
Sooner this heart ſhall bleed, which ſtill retains
The ſacred ſtamp and duty of a ſon.

S E M I R A M I S.   [falling on her knees.]

Behold thy mother kneeling on the earth
Entreats her ſon to ſtrike, and to appeaſe
The manes of great Ninus!—Gracious powers,
What is't I ſee ? thy tears mingling with mine !
O day replete with horror and with tranſport !
Yet, Ninias, ere thou giv'ſt the death I aſk,
Let Nature's powerful voice once more addreſs
  thee ;
Permit, at leaſt, thy guilty mother's tears
To bathe this hand, ſo fatal, ſo belov'd.

N I N I A S.   [raiſing her.]

Forget not I'm your ſon ;—it ill becomes you
T' embrace my knees, and ſue to me for pardon.
Be patient, and lay comfort to your ſoul ;
You've this day gain'd a new and loyal ſubject.
Heaven is appeas'd, and has reſtor'd your ſon.
But O, I warn you, ſacrifice Aſſures
To that relenting God who pardons thee.

S E M I R A M I S.

This goodneſs is unhoped for—yet, my ſon,

Let

Let me make fome atonement for my crimes,
And to thy hands this inftant yield that fcepter
Which has too long been fullied in my own.

N I N I A S.

Forbear! forbear! Still fhalt thou reign our
  Emprefs,
Whilft I with all the fons of Afia join
T' admire the wifdom of thy rule

S E M I R A M I S.

  It muft not be——Haft thou forgot, my fon,
What Ninus has decreed?——how he foretold
That thou fhould'ft fill my throne?——Beware, my
  fon,
How you infult his fhade!

N I N I A S.

      He fhall be foften'd
By his fon's tears, and by his wife's remorfe.
And oh! my Queen, my mother, calm thy
  grief!
And in the name of every God I charge thee
Keep fafe this fecret in thy faithful breaft,
And hide this dreadful myft'ry from the world.

END OF THE FOURTH ACT.

A C T.

ACT THE FIFTH.

SCENE THE FIRST.

An Apartment in the Palace.

SEMIRAMIS *and* OTANES *discover'd.*

OTANES.

BE comforted, O Queen!
SEMIRAMIS.

Never again
Shall peace or joy their welcome vifit pay
To guilt like mine.
Say, is that wretch Aſſures yet inform'd
Of all theſe ſtrange events ?——and do my people
Know that Arzaces is their long-loſt prince ?

OTANES.

No tongue has yet reveal'd the horrid ſecret.
The people, as ſome oracle, adore
The ſhade of Ninus; but they ſtrive in vain
To fathom its impenetrable meaning,
And proſtrate at the altars they remain,
Till yonder tomb ſhall ope its pond'rous jaws
T' admit the prince——who with the holy pontiff
Entreats the gods to fortify his arm,
And grant him power to ſtrike the unknown
victim.

SEMIRAMIS.

SEMIRAMIS.

But where's Affures, and the fair Azema?

OTANES.

With horror in her looks, death in her eyes,
Azema wanders near the facred tomb,
And ever and anon in fervent prayers
Entreats great Jove to fhield her dear Arzaces.

SEMIRAMIS.

O fhade of my dead lord! thou read'ft my heart,
Thou fee'ft that tho' 'twas pitylefs towards thee,
It boafts at leaft the feelings of a mother.

[*Exit* Otanes.

SCENE THE SECOND.

To her enter AZEMA *haftily.*

AZEMA.

Forgive me, gracious Queen, if I prefume
To rufh into your prefence.——This fad heart
Is rack'd with doubts and agonizing fears,
Permit me then to fall thus at your feet.

[*Kneels.*

SEMIRAMIS.

Rife, princefs, rife, and fpeak your pious wifhes.

AZEMA.

O fnatch a hero from impending danger,
Step between him and guilt, and fave Arzaces!

SEMIRAMIS.

Arzaces! what of him?——thou raveft.

9   AZEMA.

AZEMA.

This day
I know he is deftin'd to become your hufband.

SEMIRAMIS.

I wed Arzaces!
O ye immortal gods——

AZEMA.

Ev'n now the prieft
Prepares the nuptial rites——

SEMIRAMIS.

Thefe rites are dreadful,
Arzaces is——but fpeak—my blood runs cold.
Be quick, and name thefe dangers.——

AZEMA.

Mighty Emprefs,
You know that at this hour—the demi-god,
At thought of whom I fhudder—doth expect
A fecret facrifice fhould be perform'd
In yon dark labyrinth to Ninus facred.
And even now that impious wretch Affures
Doth rend the holy cerements of the tomb,
And dares to violate that fanctuary
Never as yet by mortal foot profaned.

SEMIRAMIS.

How know'ft thou this?—Say, wherefore fhould
        Affures
Thus dare t' infult my hufband's facred afhes,
And brave th' infernal Powers?

AZEMA.

AZEMA.

——For a vile one.
Eternal night reigns in these dreadful caverns,
Hid in the friendly covert of whose darkness,
He means to raise his sacrilegious hand
Against the sacred life of his new monarch.

SEMIRAMIS.

What spectre, or what god reveal'd this deed?

AZEMA.

Deep-searching love has probed his dark de-
signs.——
E'en now the monster's boldly marching on
To sacrilege and murder.——Thro' the city
He's caused it to be rumour'd that Arzaces
Is the devoted victim——in whose death
Ninus will wash away his mighty wrongs.

SEMIRAMIS.

Thou hast no cause for fear——virtue like thine
The gods themselves protect——sure thou may'st
trust
A parent's care and fondness.——Lov'd Azema,
This instant both our fates shall be accomplish'd.
Haste, pious maid, and supplicate great Jove
To shield Arzaces——whilst I fly to save
Your husband and my son.

AZEMA.

O mighty pow'rs,
What is't I hear !——Is then Arzaces Ninias?

K   SEMIRAMIS.

SEMIRAMIS.

The gods themselves enlighten'd my dark soul
When they beheld me plunging into crimes.
Once more methinks they inspire a wretched
     mother,
And in their endless mercy deign to shed
Soft peace and new-born joy on my sad heart.
They bid me fly to save a much-lov'd son,
And free him from a dark assassin's toils.

                     [*Exit* Semiramis.

Manet A Z E M A.

What sudden cause thus animates the Queen ?
What are her great designs ? why does her heart
Thus heave and swell as it would burst her
     breast ?
This prodigy surpasses all my hopes.
The prince is found ! O blest, yet fearful ti-
     dings !
My fond love whispers, that his anxious mother
Will come too late to shield him from the trai-
     tor.
O why, ye cruel gods, was he restor'd,
Thus soon to tear him from my bleeding heart.

                     [*Exit* Azema.

                     SCENE

SCENE THE THIRD,

*Changes to the Mausoleum, and the Queen re-enters,
arm'd with a Sword.*

SEMIRAMIS.

Shade of immortal Ninus! lo I come
Prepar'd t' avenge thy manes——for behold
The fatal hour is now arriv'd, in which
Thou did'ft thyself declare it should be lawful
For me to penetrate this dark abode.
Still am I bound t' obey thee; and these hands,
Which heretofore have held the reins of empire,
At thy command are arm'd to aid thy son.
     O mighty Jove,
Thou know'ft the purity of my intents,
'Tis thine t' affift me in this hour of terror.
     [Enters the Mausoleum.

SCENE THE FOURTH.

Enter NINIAS *and* AZEMA.

AZEMA.

Do I behold you once again in safety,
And in these arms enfold the son of Ninus!
My long-loft sovereign, and my deftin'd spouse?
NINIAS.
Yes, my belov'd Azema, you embrace
    K 2   Your

Your long betroth'd, your ever faithful prince.
Yet know, this blood curdles within these veins,
The dreadful mystery has been reveal'd ;
And lo ! I tremble now to know myself.
Dispel these horrors, that surround my soul !
Strengthen my heart, and nerve this drooping arm,
Bid it revenge a father———.

AZEMA.

                    Prince, take heed
How you fulfil this dreadful oracle.

NINIAS.

From me the gods demand a sacrifice,
I've sworn, and must obey.

AZEMA.

                    And canst thou think
Ninus requires his son should prove the victim ?

NINIAS.

I understand thee not———

AZEMA.

                    Thou shalt not enter
Into yon house of darkness—there a traitor
Ev'n at this instant spreads a deadly snare,
And by a coward's plan means to destroy
His unsuspecting prince.

NINIAS.

                    Shall I not enter ?
No pow'r on earth shall stay me—nought deter me.

AZEMA.

AZEMA. [*kneeling.*]

Thus humbly on my knees let me implore thee
To hear and take my counsel—base Assures
With sacrilegious steps doth violate
Thy father's sacred tomb, and there ev'n now,
Arm'd like a dark assassin, he awaits
To lift his rebel arm against thy life !

NINIAS.

Great Gods, all is reveal'd ! 'tis ye who've dragg'd
Forth to the light these deeds of guilt and dark-
    ness !
My fears are now remov'd, my victim's known.
And hark ! my father, by this monster poison'd,
Now cries aloud, and doth demand his blood.
Instructed by the priest, led on by Jove,
By Ninus' self thus arm'd—within yon tomb
Fearless I'll strike the blow, and yield to Fate.
        [*Enters the tomb.*

SCENE THE FIFTH.

AZEMA.

May every guardian pow'r shield and protect him,
And guide his steps in yon dark cave of death !
Ye horrid caverns, ye whose dreadful wombs
Brought forth dead Ninus ! once again yawn wide,
And be the victim murderous Assures.
And thou, great Ninus, his too cruel sire,
        2   Thou

Thou who would'ft not permit his weeping mo-
    ther
T' attend him in thy tomb—war on his fide.
But foft ! methought I heard his well-known voice
Mingled with dying groans.   [*It thunders.*
Hark ! the loud thunder rolls, vindictive lightnings
Inflame the heav'ns, and fhake the guilty earth,
Yet I'm not loft to hope—See where he comes !
The conqueror—the avenger !

SCENE THE SIXTH.

It thunders and lightens.

NINIAS.
              Ye gods ! where am I ?
AZEMA.
Alas ! my lord, horror fits on your brow,
You're breathlefs, pale, and bloody.
NINIAS.
                'Tis the blood
Of that vile parricide who flaughter'd Ninus.
My father was my guide, his facred fhade
Mark'd where I fhould perform this act of juftice.
Behind a pillar, one funereal lamp
Darting its feeble ray, fcarce yielded light
Sufficient to behold the glittering fword
Which bafe Affures brandifh'd, whilft his arm
                Trembled

Trembled thro' guilt—and I with tenfold rage
Twice plung'd my vengeful steel deep in his breast,
Still was revenge unfated; and my arm,
Dyed in the affaffin's blood, with fury dragg'd
    him
Near to the entrance of the gloomy cavern.

            A Z E M A.

Say, wherefore have you left his impure corfe
Within thofe hallow'd walls?

            N I N I A S.

               Belov'd Azema,
I muft confefs the traitor's deep-fetch'd groans,
Which feem'd at this laft hour to rend his heart,
Unftrung my nerves, forc'd me to quit my prey,
And to abandon my ftill-bleeding victim.
But fay, Azema, wherefore is my foul,
Tho' pure and undefil'd, yet chill'd with fear?
Wherefore am I ftill deftin'd to endure
The pangs of keen remorfe?

            A Z E M A.

             Fear not, brave prince!
The deed was pleafing to the gods—at length
The demons of revenge are fatisfied,
And Ninus' reftlefs fpirit fleeps in peace.
And, fince the curft Affures is no more——

      [Affures *appears at the farther End of the*
        Stage, with fome of his Party.

                  N I N I A S.

N I N I A S.

Juft Gods! what do I fee? that hateful traitor
Living, and in my prefence!———
What act has then my erring hand perform'd?
Now will I drag thee to my father's tomb,
And there, as he commanded, will perform
That facrifice ordain'd by Jove himfelf.

A S S U R E S.

Know I defpife thy threats, fcoff at thy vengeance.
My greateft torment I endure already,
'Tis to view thee my fovereign.

[*Exit* Azema.

[*They fight, and* Affures *falls.*]

Yet, fond youth,
I leave thee far more wretched——fee yon tomb!
Look and contemplate thy late glorious act! [*Dies.*
[Semiramis, *appears wounded, leaning on a
Prieft, at the Entrance of the Tomb.*

N I N I A S.

O horror! horror! has my blinded rage
Struck at my mother?

Enter O R O E S *and* A Z E M A.

O R O E S.

Prince, hafte to the temple,
And at the altars purify thofe hands,
Whilft you replace in mine that fatal blade
Which Heav'n ordain'd its inftrument of ven-
geance.

N I N I A S.

NINIAS.

Off!—let me plunge it in my guilty breaft!

SEMIRAMIS.

O much-lov'd fon, hafte to revenge my death;
For in thy father's tomb I'm fall'n the prey
To an affaffin's facrilegious hand!

NINIAS.

O hour of horror! O unheard-of crimes!
That facrilegious monfter was thy fon.
But I will follow thee down to the tomb,
And thou fhalt die reveng'd.—

SEMIRAMIS.

Alas, my child!
Into that houfe of darknefs I defcended
To fave thy precious life, thy wretched mother
Went thither to defend and to affift thee;
But O unerring juftice! I've receiv'd
From thy dear hands that death I've long deferv'd.

NINIAS.

This deed fhall prove the laft accurfed act
Of my loath'd life—I call the gods to witnefs,
Thofe cruel gods who led me on to murder———

SEMIRAMIS.

It is enough—I pardon thee my death,
If thy dear hands will deign to clofe my eyes.
Come to thefe arms! I crave it in the name
Of that fame blood from which thou fprang'ft,
which now

L   In

In purple tides flows from thy mother's heart.
O my lov'd son, let us exchange forgiveneſs!
Thy will conducted not thy cruel hand,
And lo, I'm juſtly puniſh'd.——My ſon!—Azema!
Let your expiring mother join your hands.
May ye live long, bleſt in each other's goodneſs ;
And may your reign be proſperous as 'tis juſt !
Ah! now death haſtens on, I feel him now
Thro' all my ſenſes—O farewell, my ſon,
My deareſt ſon !—O mercy, mercy, Heav'n !
It's paſt—it's finiſh'd.——Oh !   [*She dies.*

N I N I A S.

Farewell much-lov'd, yet O too guilty mother !
Let the remembrance of thy crimes, O Queen,
Sleep with thee in the tomb, while thy great deeds
Live in the boſom of thy mournful ſon.

O R O E S.

Such ſad examples ſhould inſtruct mankind,
The higher they are plac'd in this bad world
The ſtricter they are call'd to their account,
The more ſeverely puniſh'd.——O that all, then,
Wou'd ſet due bounds to fierce o'erbearing paſſion,
And ſeek the paths of never-erring virtue !
Then ſhould they meet a bright reward on earth,
With peace, and joys ineffable hereafter.

END OF THE FIFTH ACT.

EPILOGUE.

EPILOGUE.

Written by R. B. SHERIDAN, Esq;

Spoken by Mrs. YATES.

Dishevell'd still, like Asia's bleeding Queen,
   Shall I with jests deride the tragic scene?
No, beauteous mourners!—from whose downcast eyes—
The Muse has drawn her noblest sacrifice!
Whose gentle bosoms, Pity's altars—bear
The chrystal incense of each falling tear!—
—There lives the Poet's praise!—no critic art·
Can match the comment of a feeling heart!
   When gen'ral plaudits speak the Fable o'er—
Which mute attention had approv'd before,
Tho' ruder spirits love th' accustom'd jest
Which chases sorrow from the vulgar breast,
Still hearts refin'd their sadden'd tint retain—
—The sigh is pleasure! and the jest is pain!—
—Scarce have they smiles to honour Grace or Wit,
—Tho' Roscius spoke the verse himself had writ!
Thus thro' the time when vernal fruits receive
The grateful show'rs that hang on April's eve;
Tho' ev'ry coarser stem of forest birth
Throws with the morning-beam its dews to earth,
—Ne'er does the gentle Rose revive so soon—
But bath'd in Nature's tears, it droops till noon.
                           O could

EPILOGUE.

O could the Muſe one ſimple moral teach,
From ſcenes like theſe, which all who heard might
    reach!
—Thou child of Sympathy—whoe'er thou art,
Who with Aſſyria's Queen haſt wept thy part—
Go ſearch, where keener woes demand relief,
Go—while thy heart yet beats with fancy'd grief,
Thy lip ſtill conſcious of the recent ſigh,
The graceful tear ſtill ling'ring in thy eye—
Go—and on real miſery beſtow
The bleſt effuſion of fictitious woe!—

So ſhall our Muſe, ſupreme of all the Nine,
Deſerve, indeed, the title of—Divine!—
Virtue ſhall own her favour'd from above,
And PITY *—greet her—with a ſiſter's love!*

F I N I S.

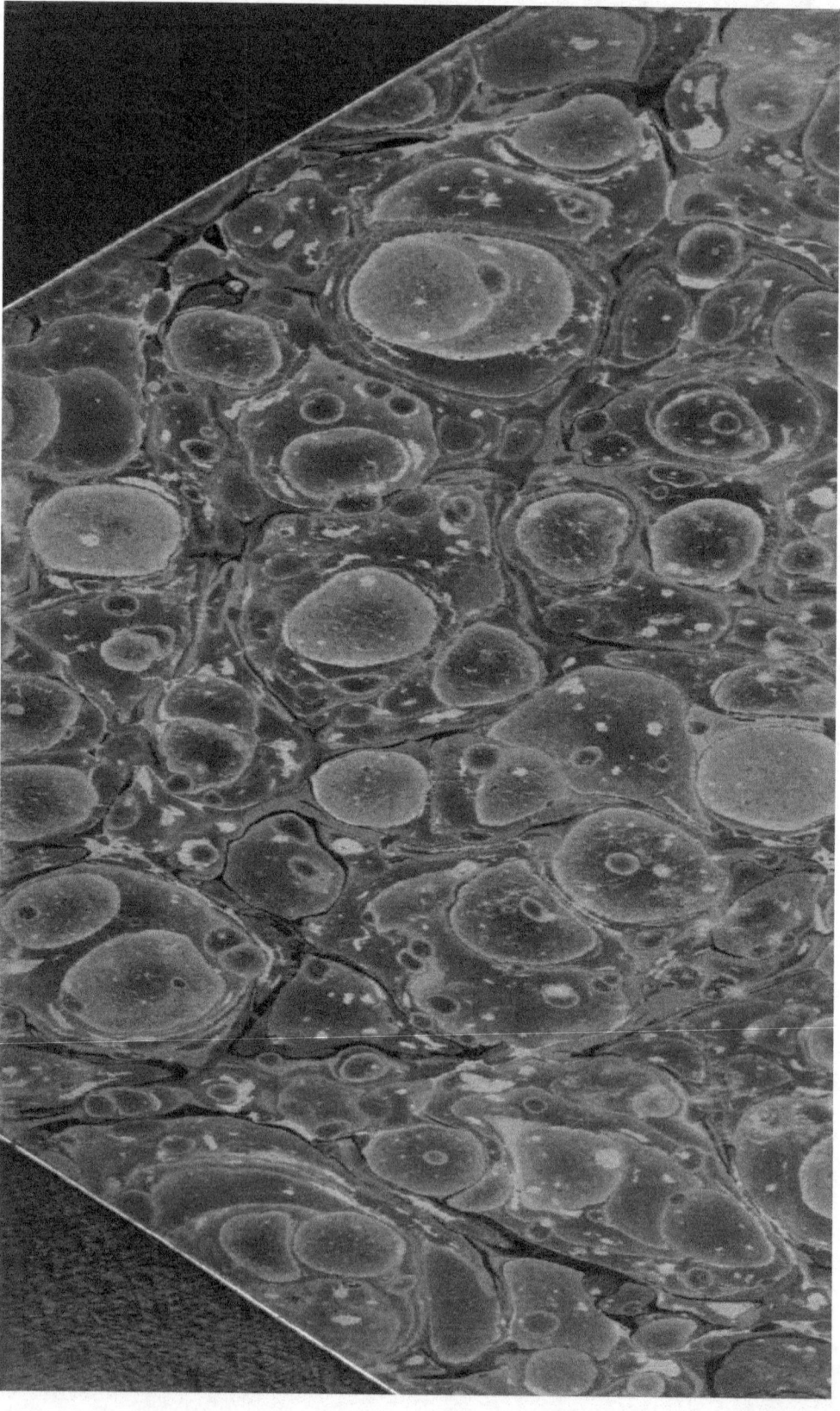

Check Out More Titles From HardPress Classics Series In this collection we are offering thousands of classic and hard to find books. This series spans a vast array of subjects – so you are bound to find something of interest to enjoy reading and learning about.

Subjects:
Architecture
Art
Biography & Autobiography
Body, Mind &Spirit
Children & Young Adult
Dramas
Education
Fiction
History
Language Arts & Disciplines
Law
Literary Collections
Music
Poetry
Psychology
Science
…and many more.

Visit us at www.hardpress.net